BRIGHT IDEA BOOKS

AMAZING Volcanoes AROUND THE WORLD

by Simon Rose

Raintree is an imprint of Capstone Global Library Limited, a company incorporated in England and Wales having its registered office at 264 Banbury Road, Oxford, OX2 7DY – Registered company number: 6695582

www.raintree.co.uk
myorders@raintree.co.uk

Edited by Claire Vanden Branden
Designed by Becky Daum
Original illustrations © Capstone Global Library Limited 2020
Production by Dan Peluso
Originated by Capstone Global Library Ltd
Printed and bound in India

ISBN 978 1 4747 7469 7 (hardback)
ISBN 978 1 4747 8122 0 (paperback)

British Library Cataloguing in Publication Data
A full catalogue record for this book is available from the British Library.

Acknowledgements
We would like to thank the following for permission to reproduce photographs: Alamy: Aurora Photos, 21, 22–23; iStockphoto: RomanKhomlyak, 10–11; Newscom: World History Archive, 9; Shutterstock Images: Adrian Baker, 5, Bos11, 6–7, 28, Bryan Busovicki, 18–19, Erdem Summak, 26–27, Georgia Carini, 14–15, Kanjanee Chaisin, cover, Putu Artana, 25, Ralf Lehmann, 17, 31, Wead, 13.

CONTENTS

CHAPTER 1

AMAZING
Volcanoes

A volcano is a type of mountain. Most volcanoes have hot liquid rock inside them. This melted rock is called **magma**. It comes from deep inside Earth.

When magma breaks through Earth's surface it becomes **lava**.

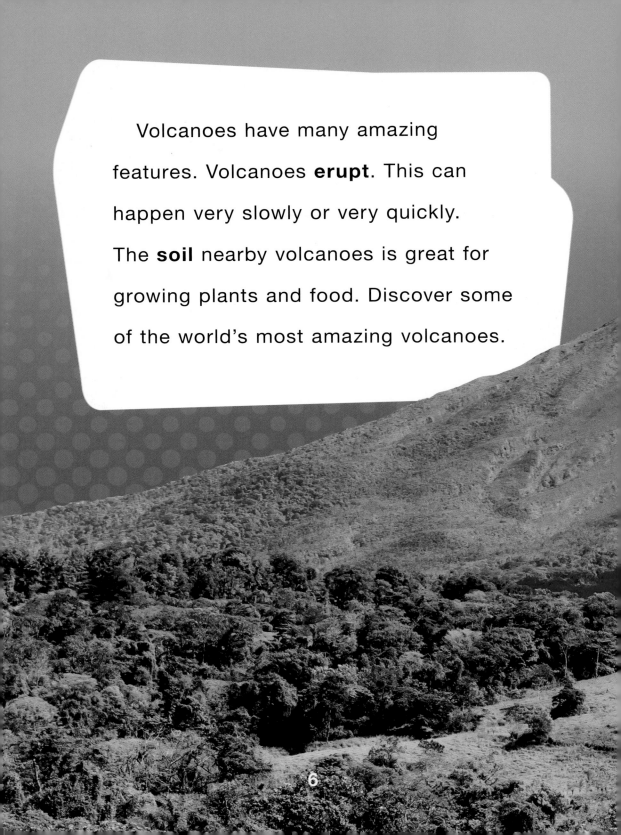

Volcanoes have many amazing features. Volcanoes **erupt**. This can happen very slowly or very quickly. The **soil** nearby volcanoes is great for growing plants and food. Discover some of the world's most amazing volcanoes.

There are approximately 1,500 volcanoes on Earth that could erupt.

CHAPTER 2

MOUNT St. Helens

Mount St. Helens is near Seattle, Washington, in the United States. It is 2,550 metres (8,365 feet) high.

Mount St. Helens was shaped like a cone. On 18 May 1980 the volcano erupted and the cone was blasted away.

Nearly 14 per cent of the volcano was destroyed. Gas and rock sprayed into the air.

Mount St. Helens's 1980 eruption is the deadliest eruption in the history of the United States.

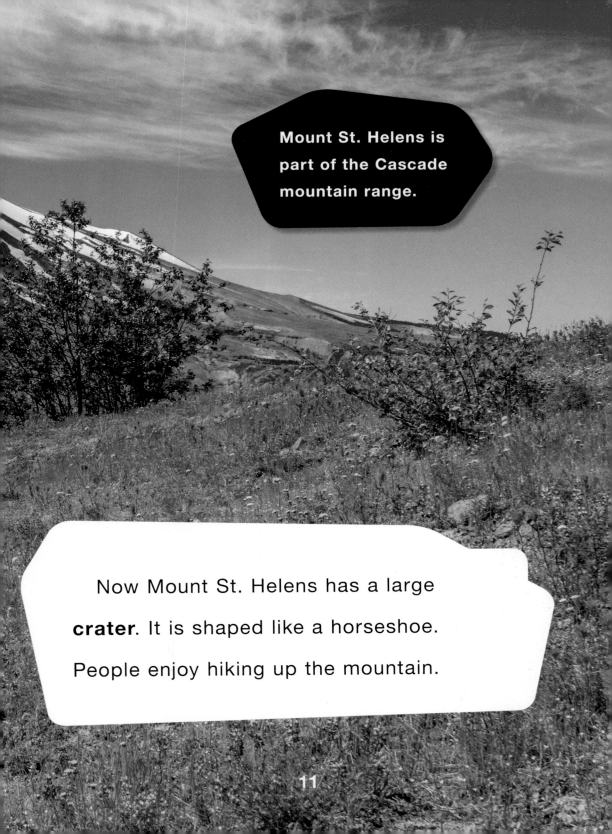

Mount St. Helens is part of the Cascade mountain range.

Now Mount St. Helens has a large **crater**. It is shaped like a horseshoe. People enjoy hiking up the mountain.

CHAPTER 3

MOUNT
Etna

Mount Etna is in Italy. It is 3,329 metres (10,900 feet) high and is the largest **active** volcano in Europe. Lava often flows from this volcano.

Mount Etna can shoot lava high into the air.

13

TASTY FOOD

The lava makes the soil good for growing food. Tasty grapes and olives grow here. People say they taste unlike any other olives and grapes in the world.

MOUNT VESUVIUS

Mount Vesuvius is also in Italy. In AD 79 it erupted and destroyed a city called Pompeii. Thousands of people died.

Italians are proud of the grapes they grow near Mount Etna.

CHAPTER 4

KILAUEA

Kilauea is on the island of Hawaii in the United States. It is 1,277 metres (4,190 feet) high. It is one of the most active volcanoes in the world. Its name means "much spewing" in Hawaiian.

Lava can flow many kilometres away from the volcano.

17

Kilauea often has smoke coming from its craters.

Kilauea continuously erupted from 1983 to 2018. It has more than 24 craters. Most volcanoes only have one.

MAUNA LOA

Mauna Loa is also in Hawaii. It is the largest active volcano on Earth. It is 4,169 m (13,677 feet) above sea level.

CHAPTER 5

MOUNT Erebus

Mount Erebus is in Antarctica. It is 3,793 metres (12,444 feet) high.

It has a lava lake. The lake may be many kilometres deep. It is one of only a few lava lakes in the world.

The lava lake on Mount Erebus is inside a crater.

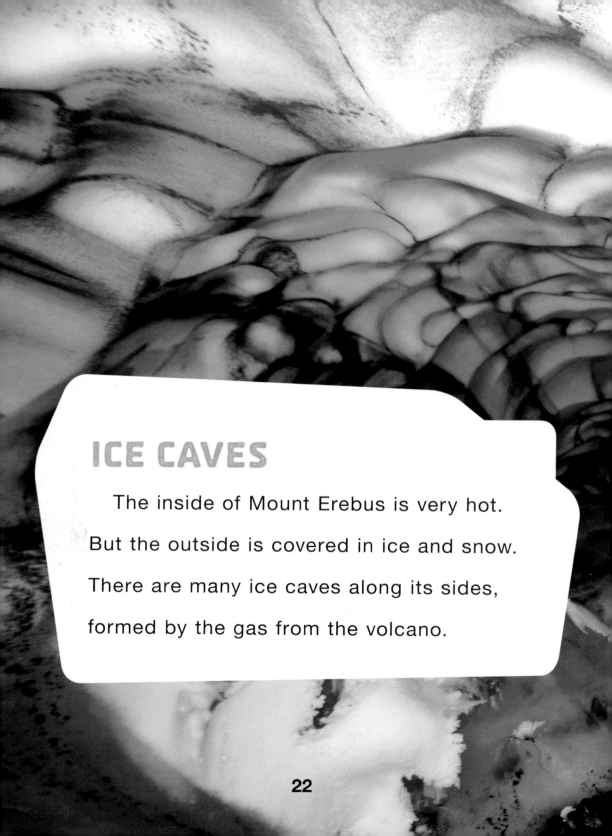

ICE CAVES

The inside of Mount Erebus is very hot.
But the outside is covered in ice and snow.
There are many ice caves along its sides,
formed by the gas from the volcano.

The ice caves along Mount Erebus are huge.

CHAPTER 6

MOUNT Agung

Mount Agung is in Bali, Indonesia. It is 3,014 metres (9,888 feet) high. It is the tallest point on the island. It is made of many layers of ash and lava.

MOUNT BROMO

Mount Bromo is also in Indonesia. People come from all over the world to see it. It is known for its views of beautiful sunrises.

Mount Agung towers over Bali.

Mount Agung is very unsafe. It is one of the world's deadliest volcanoes. Its eruptions shoot rock and ash many kilometres away. Sometimes people don't escape.

LOUDEST SOUND

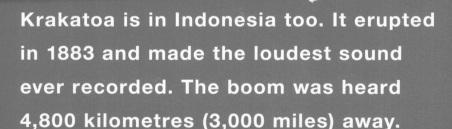

Krakatoa is in Indonesia too. It erupted in 1883 and made the loudest sound ever recorded. The boom was heard 4,800 kilometres (3,000 miles) away.

Mount Agung's deadliest eruption was in 1963.

GLOSSARY

active
way to describe a volcano that has erupted within the last 10,000 years

crater
area shaped like a bowl around the opening of a volcano

erupt
burst out with great force

lava
hot liquid rock that comes out of a volcano when it erupts

magma
melted rock underneath Earth's surface

soil
material in which plants grow

TOP
VOLCANOES
TO VISIT

KILAUEA, HAWAII, USA
Experience this continuously erupting volcano.

MOUNT AGUNG, INDONESIA
Visit the tallest point on Bali.

MOUNT EREBUS, ANTARCTICA
Take in the sights of this volcano's lava lake.

MOUNT ETNA, ITALY
Visit the largest active volcano in Europe.

MOUNT ST. HELENS, WASHINGTON, USA
See this volcano's horseshoe-shaped crater.

ACTIVITY

MAKE A VOLCANO!

Use modelling clay to make your own volcano. Mould the clay to make a shape that looks like a mountain. Make sure you leave a crater at the top. Now you can watch it erupt!

WHAT YOU'LL NEED:

- 1 teaspoon of bicarbonate of soda
- ½ cup of white vinegar
- a few drops of red or orange food colouring

INSTRUCTIONS:

Pour the bicarbonate of soda into your volcano's crater. Add the food colouring. Then pour the vinegar on top of the bicarbonate of soda. Watch your volcano erupt!

FIND OUT MORE

Books

DKfindout! Volcanoes, DK (DK Children, 2016)

Volcanoes (Learning about Landforms), Chris Oxlade (Raintree, 2015)

Volcanologist (The Coolest Jobs on the Planet), Melanie Waldron and Hugh Tuffen (Raintree, 2014)

Websites

www.bbc.com/bitesize/articles/zd9cxyc

Learn more about volcanoes. Watch a video and test your knowledge!

www.dkfindout.com/uk/earth/volcanoes

Find out more about volcanoes.

INDEX